AuthorHouse™
1663 Liberty Drive
Bloomington, IN 47403
www.authorhouse.com
Phone: 1-800-839-8640

Published by AuthorHouse 09/24/2012

ISBN: 978-1-4772-7178-0 (sc)
*   978-1-4772-7179-7 (e)*

Library of Congress Control Number: 2012917355

Any people depicted in stock imagery provided by Thinkstock are models,
and such images are being used for illustrative purposes only.
Certain stock imagery © Thinkstock.

This book is printed on acid-free paper.

author**HOUSE**®

All About Computers

Written by: L. Philippe Rodriguez

Illustrated by: Sean Miner

FunFactsBot

Dedicated to Donette A. Francis
& Xavier I. Rodriguez

All About Computers

by

L. Philippe Rodriguez

... to paying for groceries
at the Supermarket...

...to robots filling
prescriptions at
the Pharmacy...

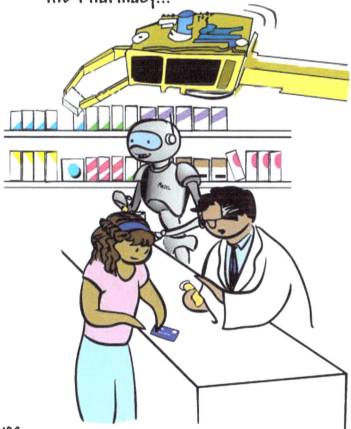

Computers play an important role in our lives.

Computers are electronic machines that perform tasks according to a set of instructions (programs).

At work, they are used to keep records, analyze data, do research, and manage projects.

Computers have 4 basic functions:
INPUT, PROCESSING, STORAGE, and OUTPUT

PROCESSING

INPUT

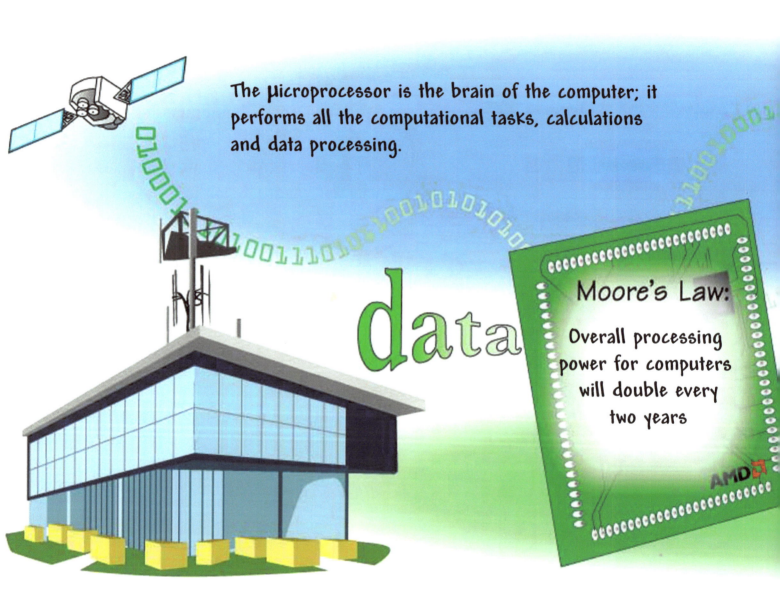

The μicroprocessor is the brain of the computer; it performs all the computational tasks, calculations and data processing.

data

Moore's Law:

Overall processing power for computers will double every two years

AMD

The group of 12 engineers who designed the IBM PC was called 'The Dirty Dozen'!

Computers are made of **Hardware and Software**

If you can touch it, it is hardware;

if you can't, it is software.

Software tells the hardware what to do and how to do it

There are two types of software:
Systems and Applications

Another name for a Microsoft Windows tutorial is 'Crash Course'!

23

Spreadsheets

Systems Software (OS) are programs that control the operations of the hardware – Android, Windows 8, iOS ...

Computer Games

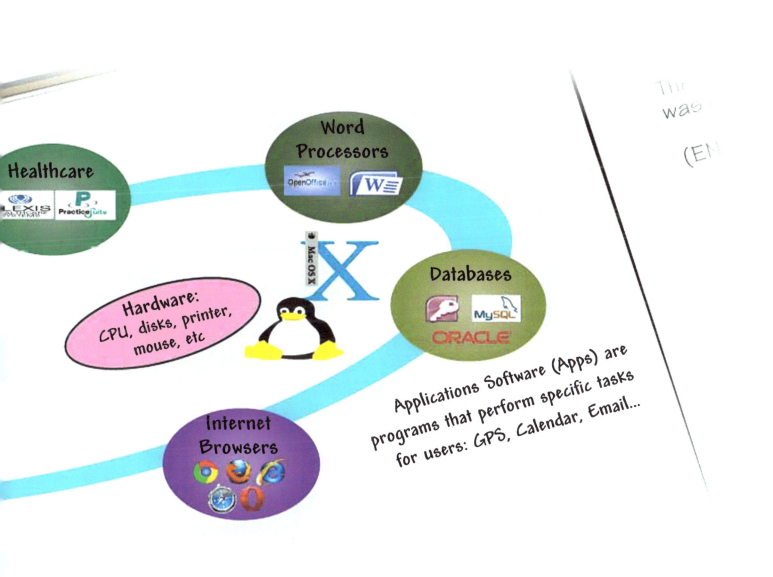

Applications Software (Apps) are programs that perform specific tasks for users: GPS, Calendar, Email...

At home, we use computers to find information, store pictures and music, track finances, play games, and stay in touch with friends and family.

Computers

Discover the infinite possibilities.

Innovate, get excited and make things.
Have fun. Build a Robot!

www.ingramcontent.com/pod-product-compliance
Lightning Source LLC
Chambersburg PA
CBHW041426050326

40689CB00002B/676